A
WINDOW
ON
THE
PAST

Early Native American Dress from the
John Painter Collection

A
WINDOW
ON
THE
PAST

by John W. Painter

—

Cincinnati Art Museum

Frontispiece: Shield, Crow, about 1870 or earlier; buffalo rawhide

This publication was funded in part by support from the August A. Rendigs, Jr. Foundation, W. Roger Fry, Trustee, and from The Chemed Corporation.

Design and topography by Noel Martin
Photography by Scott Hisey
Content editor, Glenn Markoe
Set in Sabon and Time Script by Linda Sanders, Red Bank Communications
Production manager, Howard Wells
Copy editor, Karen Feinberg
Printed by The C.J.Krehbiel Company, Cincinnati, Ohio

Library of Congress Cataloging-in-Publication Data

Painter, John W.
A window on the past: early Native American dress from the John Painter collection/John W. Painter; [photography by Scott Hisey].
p. cm.
Catalog of an exhibition.
ISBN 0-931537-24-X
1. Indians of North America–Clothing–Exhibition. 2. Painter, John W.–Ethnological collections–Exhibitions. I. Hisey, Scott. II. Cincinnati Art Museum. III. Title
E983.C8 P35 2002
391'.0089'97–dc21

2002013381

The Cincinnati Art Museum gratefully acknowledges the generous operating support provided annually by the Greater Cincinnati Fine Arts Fund, the Ohio Arts Council and the City of Cincinnati, and the Institute of Museum and Library Services.

Exhibition dates, Cincinnati Art Museum
October 13, 2002 through March 30, 2003

Foreword

The study of the history of art is, almost by definition, a collaborative enterprise, involving the efforts of scholars, curators, and collectors. This is especially true of Native American art – a field to which museums and art historians have, until relatively recently, given insufficient attention. In this regard, the efforts of passionate and discerning collectors such as John Painter have been critical in helping to advance our knowledge of the artistic traditions of native North America by assembling collections of great historical and aesthetic significance.

The Painter Collection, highlights of which are presented here in *A Window on the Past: Early Native American Dress from the John Painter Collection*, is rich in materials from the Plains and the Northern Woodlands, especially in those articles of clothing and accessories on which Native American artists lavished so much care. It is, moreover, constituted in large measure of rare, early material, with many objects dating to the late eighteenth and early nineteenth centuries. As such the Painter Collection can serve – like the exhibition with which it is being presented, *Uncommon Legacies: Masterworks of Native American Art from the Peabody Essex Museum* – as a superb resource for the study of Native American art during the period in which European and then American explorers and traders came increasingly into contact with the indigenous peoples of this continent.

It is, in sum, rare that an opportunity to present works of such exceptional quality and importance presents itself. And for this reason, the staff and Board of Trustees of the Cincinnati Art Museum are deeply grateful to Mr. Painter for his willingness to share his collection with audiences here in Cincinnati. Throughout the process of developing this exhibition and the accompanying catalogue which he has authored, he has been unfailingly generous, providing access to the rich body of documentation he has assembled during years of research. I would also like to express our thanks to the August A. Rendigs, Jr. Foundation for the financial support it has given to the production of this catalogue; to the KnowledgeWorks Foundation for its support for educational programming; and to the Western & Southern Foundation for is generous sponsorship of the exhibition. I would also like to acknowledge the contribution of Noel Martin, who provided the elegant design for this publication.

Many members of the Museum's staff deserve mention for the contributions they have made to the success of this project: Michael Brechner, our chief designer and his staff; Katie Haigh and the members of our Registration Department; Ted Lind, Marion Rauch, and Amber Lucero Criswell of the Education Division; Jackie Reau and the staff of the Marketing Division; Jill Barry and the staff of the Development Division; and Stephen Bonadies, our Deputy Director. Above all, our thanks are due to Scott Hisey, Museum Photographic Services Coordinator, for his superb photography of the objects presented in the catalogue; and to Dr. Glenn Markoe, who, as curator in charge of our Native American collections, has overseen the work of developing the exhibition and catalogue of works from the Painter Collection with great thoughtfulness and care.

— Timothy Rub, Director

Introduction

For thirty-five years I have been actively involved in collecting American Indian artifacts. These artistic achievements do credit to a people who lived a fascinating way of life that essentially ceased to exist around 1880. This catalog depicts sixty-five items from my collection, almost all of which were made before the Battle of the Little Big Horn on June 25, 1876. This famous confrontation resulted from a decree by the United States Government that Native Americans should be forcibly detained on reservations. This edict took away their freedom and destroyed their soul, pride, heritage, and sense of values – those special qualities that made the Indian so interesting and their art so distinctive.

During the "Historic Period" (about 1600-1850 A.D.) and prior to the domination of North America by the "White Man," it is estimated that there were about 2,000,000 Native Americans in over 800 tribes. It is necessary to know a great deal about these cultures in order to understand what influenced their art and artifacts. This is certainly a complicated and time-consuming task. Indians found it necessary to develop a sign language system to simplify communications, since nearly all of the 800 tribes spoke a different language. Even then, interpreters were necessary, because sign language could be undecipherable to a novice. Only the Cherokee had an alphabet that had 86 letters and was devised by their renowned leader, Sequoyah, in about 1820. Under these conditions, pictographic art was a natural development.

The pre-reservation cultures of Native Americans have much to admire. I do not agree with those authors who describe Native Americans as "savages." It is dangerous to generalize, but most: (1) were religious and believed that a supreme being created the sky, earth, and underworld – and that there is an afterlife in the "Happy Hunting Ground"; (2) respected the authority of their leaders and cared for their elders; (3) loved children, who were trained and cared for by many members of the tribe in addition to their parents; (4) believed that touching an enemy (counting coup) was more worthy of recognition than killing. (Lying was severely punished and honesty was demanded while recounting acts of bravery and past deeds.); (5) had a societal structure which incorporated many groupings that were very similar to our clubs of today; (6) had learned to cope with the forces of nature and the environment that literally surrounded them, since they spent most of their lives outside; (7) shared the earth with animals, insects, birds, and fish in a degree of harmony. They had a strong kinship with and held great respect for the special abilities and traits of these creatures.

My primary criterion for selecting objects for my collection is that quality has no substitute. One great item hanging on a wall looks great; fifty mediocre items hanging on a wall look mediocre. Age does not insure quality; provenance does not insure quality; rarity does not insure quality. If we first demand that an object is of quality, we can then be pleased if it also has age, provenance, or rarity. I make a great effort to acquire works that were made prior to 1850, and I believe that 40 of the 65 items in my exhibition fall into this category. In 1976, Ted J. Brasser, a noted authority on Native American art, observed in *Bo'jou Neejee! Profiles of Canadian Indian Art*: "Pre-1850 Indian artifacts are extremely rare in ethnographic museums, where they are considered the irreplaceable treasures of the collections." In 1965, Norman Feder stated in his catalog *American Indian Art Before 1850*: "Pre-1850 Indian artifacts are not common in American museums. In general, a museum will consider itself fortunate to possess a dozen specimens and still more fortunate, if they are documented."

I am pleased to be a part of this fine exhibition and hope that you will find these objects to be interesting and educational.

— John Painter

1. Costume: Coat, Leggings, Mittens

Cree, about 1780
Native tanned hide, probably caribou or moose (coat and mittens), young deer or antelope (leggings), porcupine quills, dyed horsehair, wool cloth, blanket cloth, metal buttons (Hudson's Bay Company), glass beads (pony, tubular, ovoid, and barleycorn), sinew, pigment
L (coat): 47 in.; L (leggings): 30 in.; L (mittens): 9½ in.; Diameter (buttons): 27/32 in.
Provenance. Major Edward Barwick, England, early 19th century. (Following extended military service in America, Barwick took this costume home to England after the War of 1812; it descended in the Barwick family until purchased for the Painter Collection in October 1991, from Miss Janet Farrar, Leeds, England. The grandmother of Miss Farrar's father was a Barwick before marriage.)

This type of coat is documented in 14 museums and two private collections. Along with an example in the National Museum of Ireland in Dublin (acc. no. 1892.20; pub. Glenbow Museum, *The Spirit Sings* (1987) 76 (illus.)), it displays a level of artistic achievement rarely seen in Native American craftwork.

The paints used to decorate this costume were made from the roe of various fish and from other pigments. The paint was pressed into hide with a bone "brush" that made an indentation or trench during the painting process. The mittens have beaded hangs on the inside edge along the forefinger because they attracted more attention in this position than along the bottom side of the little finger area.

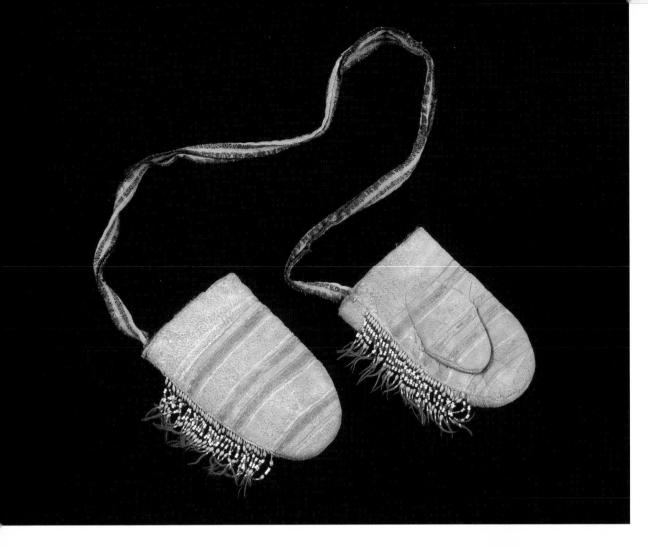

The coat has four brass buttons with eyelets. They bear a distinct decorative design that includes four piglike animals (actually beavers, probably created for the Hudson's Bay Company by a designer in England who had never seen this animal) divided into four quadrants by a Saint George's cross with a decorative scroll at the top (similar to the shield in the coat of arms of the Hudson's Bay Company).[1]

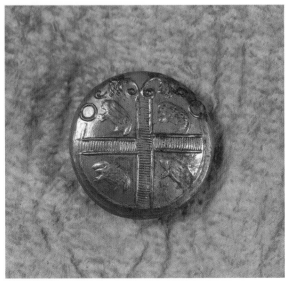

1. Fort Rivière Tremblante was built on the Upper Assiniboine River, west of Lake Winnipeg, in 1791 and was used until 1799. When it was excavated in the 1960s, an assortment of 112 buttons was found; no two were alike. One of these buttons is identical to those on my coat, and is referred to as "the famous Hudson's Bay Company beaver button." (See E. Leigh Syms and P. Smith, "Unbuttoning the History of Fort Rivière Tremblante," The Beaver (Spring 1984) 26-30.) One button is missing from my coat!

2. Warrior's Shirt

Upper Missouri River area, about 1855
Native tanned hide (probably deer), dark
blue and black glass beads, porcupine
quills, remnants of light-colored horsehair,
red and blue stroud cloth, sinew
 H:40 in.; W:56 in. (wrist to wrist)
Provenance. Will Channing, New York
City, 1985; Painter Collection, 1985.

Several characteristics help to determine an
early date of manufacture for this hide
shirt: (1) It is sinew-sewn. (2) The sides are
left open, and the skins of the animals' legs
hang down from the corners. (3) Each
piece of fringe is inserted halfway through
holes in one side of the quilled strips.
To accommodate this, the strips are made
wider on the side where the fringe is
inserted. (4) The quilled strips exhibit
certain features: three or fewer colors are
used; the red and blue crossbars are
straight lines; the blue "fingerlike" accents
are relatively short. (5) Two remnants or
hangs of light-colored horsehair are
attached with sinew wrapping to the
shoulder area. (In the "Indian Wars"
period it was customary to attach snips of
hair from a warrior's favorite warhorse.)
(6) Stroud cloth is an "over-and-under,"
two-strand woven fabric, which was used
to make the red-and-blue triangular neck
flap. A similar flap is seen on older shirts,
as in Karl Bodmer's Tableau no. 13 of
Mato Tope (Four Bears). This early cloth
was not made from dyed yarn, but was
dyed after weaving. The blue stroud on the
neck flap shows lighter areas where this
early dying process did not produce a
consistent solid blue color.[1]

---

*1. George Horse Capture, Richard A. Pohrt,
Paul Gray, Colin Taylor, Kurt Schindler, and
Herman Seeger studied this shirt in relation to
its date of manufacture and confirmed my
conclusions.*

3. Leggings

Blackfeet, about 1860-1870
Deerskin, ermine strips, glass beads,
pigment, sinew, thread
L:34 in.
Provenance. James Hooper (1897-1971),
England; Christie's, London, *Tribal Art*,
June 23,1986, Lot 6 (consigned by a
granddaughter of Hooper); Jim Hart,
Cherry Hill, New Jersey, and Alex
Acevedo, New York City, dealers, 1986;
Painter Collection, 1986.
Published. S. Phelps, *Art and Artifacts of
the Pacific, Africa, and the Americas –
The James Hooper Collection* (1976) 341,
no. 1615 (illus.) and 447 (described).

Each legging has three vertical rows of
nine tadpoles each, which are painted dark
brown; the tadpole is a symbol of fertility
for tribes of the Plains. The skin tassels
attached to one side of each legging are the
remains of ermine strips, which have lost
their hair. The beaded strips display an
overlay stitch and a stepped triangle design
that are very typical of the Blackfeet people.

4. Leggings

Great Lakes area, possibly Ottawa or Chippewa, about 1800
Wool cloth, silk ribbon, glass beads, thread
L:27 in.
Provenance. Sir John Colborne, England (born 1778), collected about 1830 and descended in the family; Sotheby's, New York, *American Indian Art*, June 4,1997, Lot 14; Painter Collection, 1997.

Wool leggings from the eighteenth/early nineteenth-century from the Great Lakes region are quite rare: only a half-dozen published examples are attested.[1] These leggings were collected in the early nineteenth century by Sir John Colborne, who served with distinction in the Revolutionary and Napoleonic Wars, and who was later known as Baron Seaton. Seaton served as Lieutenant Governor of Upper Canada (1828-1836), as commander of British forces in Upper and Lower Canada (1836-1838), and as Governor General of Canada (1838-1839), and returned to England in 1839.

1. Known examples are as follows:
(1) The New Brunswick Museum, Saint John, Maliseet, late eighteenth century. Pub. Glenbow Museum, The Spirit Sings, exh. cat. (1987) 18, no. E31. (2) The New Brunswick Museum, Micmac, early nineteenth century. Pub. The Spirit Sings, 19, no. E36. (3) Royal Ontario Museum, Ottawa, early nineteenth century. Pub. The Spirit Sings, 65, no. W128. (4) Bern Historical Museum, Switzerland, Ottawa, late eighteenth century. Pub. The Spirit Sings, 64, no. W124. (5) Berlin Museum, presumably Comanche [?], collected 1840. Pub. Native American Art, exh. cat. (1999) 56, fig. 39. (6) New York State Museum, Albany, photo in Painter Collection files. [They appear to be made of green wool cloth which is rarely used; but, when used, usually indicated an early date of manufacture.]

5. Leggings, Bottom Tab Type

Northern Plains, about 1800
Native tanned hide, glass pony beads, human hair, sinew, pigment
L:41 in. (not including fastening extensions); 56 in. (including fastening extensions). *Provenance.* Bob Vandenburg, Corrales, New Mexico, acquired about 1980 at Ohio Gun Collectors' Show, Columbus; Malcolm Grimmer, dealer, Santa Fe, n.d.; Painter Collection, 2000.

This style is called "bottom tab leggings." The blue-and-white pony-beaded leather strips sewn down the outside of each legging caused a corresponding raised area along the inside. These inside areas show heavy patination, indicating frequent use over a long period. "Pony" beads are comparatively large glass trade beads favored by Native American artists from about 1800 to 1850. They were approximately .35 centimeters in diameter and came in only a few colors: white, blue, red, black and yellow. Smaller "seed" beads in a variety of colors became available about 1850. The use of very few bead colors and the simplicity of design are features found most often on artifacts datable before 1850. The use of only blue and white beads in simple alternating squares exemplifies such early influences. These leggings are one of my favorite items.

6. Moccasins *(right)*

Cree, about 1775
Native tanned hide, porcupine quills, metal cones, dyed horsehair, sinew
L:10½ in.
Provenance. James Hooper (1897-1971), England; Christie's, London, *Important Tribal Art*, June 23, 1992, Lot 130 (consigned by the three daughters of one of Hooper's grandchildren); Painter Collection, 1992.
Published. S. Phelps, *Art and Artifacts of the Pacific, Africa, and the Americas – The James Hooper Collection* (1976) 345, no. 1636 (illus.) and 448 (described).

These moccasins probably were made by the same tribe and at approximately the same time as the Cree coat (cat. no. 1). They feature woven quillwork panels.

7. Moccasins *(left)*

Iroquois, about 1800-1830
Native tanned hide, rose-red velvet cloth,
satin hemming cloth, porcupine quills,
glass beads, sinew, thread
L:9¼ in.
Provenance. Jim Hart, dealer, Cherry Hill,
New Jersey, n.d.; Painter Collection, 1984.

The porcupine quills on this pair of
moccasins have rich, subtle hues, which
produce a warm effect and an understated
elegance. For an almost identical pair of
moccasins in the Detroit Institute of Art,
see D.W. Penny, *Art of the American
Indian Frontier, the Chandler-Pohrt
Collection* (1992) 73, no. 7 (identified as
Iroquois). Also, see K.Kramer in
*Uncommon Legacies: Native American Art
from the Peabody Essex Museum* (2002)
97, no. 21 (identified as Iroquois, early
19th century. As Kramer states, "Here,
beadwork and quill embroidery are
combined for a pleasing effect.")

8. Moccasins

Probably Seneca, about 1800
Native tanned hide, porcupine quills, glass beads, silk ribbon. All quilling appears to be sewn with a beige twisted thread.
L:9¾ in.
Provenance: Mark J.Sykes, Leeds, England, 1984 (acquired for 2 pounds at Queen's Hall, Leeds, from mother of previous owner[1]); Michael Johnson, dealer, Walsall, England, 1984; Tad Dale, dealer, London, 1984/85; Painter Collection, 1985 (purchased through Richard Edwards, Toledo, Ohio).

This is a fine example of rare, early quilled moccasins. A very similar pair, collected by Prince Maximilian zu Wied (1782-1867) in the Niagara Falls region, may be found in the Linden Museum, Stuttgart (identified as "Woodlands, ca. 1800 or before"). For an illustration of another similar pair, see Walter Krickeberg, *Baessler-Archiv. Beitrage zur Volkerkunde, neue folge band II* (Berlin 1954) pl. 22. Also, see K. Kramer in *Uncommon Legacies: Native American Art from the Peabody Essex Museum* (2002) 104, no. 27 (identified as Iroquois, early 19th century).

---

1. This provenance was provided by Mr. Sykes, who wrote to me after seeing the moccasins illustrated in J.W.Painter, American Indian Artifacts: the John Painter Collection (1992) 48, no. 29. The previous owner had originally purchased them for six pence at a «jumble sale» in northern England shortly after World War II.

9. Moccasins

Plains Cree, about 1840 or earlier
Native tanned hide (moose or deerskin)
with a vamp insert (probably caribou),
porcupine and bird quills, trade
cloth, sinew
L:9¼ in.
Provenance. E.B.Gray, Esq., Scotland,
n.d.; Christie's, New York, *Tribal Art*,
November 28,1984, Lot 102[1]; Painter
Collection, 1984.

Each vamp is a separate piece, which is
sewn into the top. A thin border of red
bird quills around the edges of the vamps
is wrapped with dark blue bird quills,
which results in an alternating red-and-
blue color spiral. Flowers are outlined
delicately with fine porcupine quilling.
Each vamp bears three small rosettes, and
the high ankle flaps have serrated edges;
neither of these is a common decoration
on Plains Indian artifacts.

---

1. *According to Christie's, the former owner,
Mr. Gray, was over ninety years old at the time
his family decided to sell his Indian artifact
collection. Both the family and auction house
were apparently concerned for his reaction to
the shock of the surprisingly high prices paid
for his small collection, which Mr. Gray
thought was of little monetary value.*

10. Moccasins

Seminole, pre-1850
Native tanned hide, glass beads, silver-plated and gold-plated metal beads, silk cloth, sinew, thread
L:9½ in.

Provenance. The Betty Sterling Collection, Honolulu, n.d.; Alexander Gallery, New York, 1988; Howard Roloff, Victoria, British Columbia, 1988; Painter Collection, 1988.

Published. Honolulu Academy of Arts, *Of Pride and Spirit: North American Indian Art from a Private Collection in Hawaii,* exh. cat (1981) 47, no. 29, the Betty Sterling Collection (incorrectly identified as Northeast Woodlands); Alexander Gallery, New York, *Something for Everyone* (Christmas 1988) 65 (incorrectly identified as Western Great Plains); M. Johnson, *American Indians of the Southeast,* Osprey Military, Men-at-Arms, Series 288 (1995) 15 (illus.); C. Taylor, *North American Indians – A Pictorial History of the Indian Tribes of North America* (1997), no.34 (illus.).

On each side of each ankle there are beaded designs of what appear to be frogs laying eggs. The inside is lined with green silk cloth. Tiny chainstitching over silk material appears on the back seam. More than 1,500 gold-plated beads form six

circles and outline the front toe area. *(See detail left.)* Silver plated beads are also used. (Gold- and silver-plated beads are rarely used on Indian artifacts.) The process for making these tiny beads, some of which are geodesic in shape, is not yet fully understood. (See J.W.Painter, *American Indian Artifacts: The John Painter Collection* (1992) 45-46.) For another pair of Southeastern moccasins that have gold beads, see J.R.Grimes in *Uncommon Legacies: Native American Art from the Peabody Essex Museum* (2002) 125, no. 41. As Grimes remarks, "The moccasins...are sumptuously decorated with blue, green, and metallic gold beads."

11. Hair Drop

Kiowa, about 1850
German silver conchas, buffalo hide strip, hide attachment thongs
L:67½ in.; Diameter (conchas): 2 15/16 in.
Provenance. Paul Gray, dealer, Old Chatham, New York, n.d,; Painter Collection, 1991

The hairdrop, an ornament worn fastened to the back of a man's head, and extending almost to the ground, was particularly popular among the Kiowa. It is referred to as early as 1832 in Kiowa "Winter Counts," and remained in fashion for a relatively short time. This example consists of a series of circular disks, or conchas, attached to a buffalo hide strip. They were made of German silver, an alloy of copper, zinc, and nickel that served as a less expensive substitute for the actual metal. Probably derived from prehistoric Southeast shell disks, they were introduced to metal smiths of the Southern Plains by tribes who were forcibly relocated in the 1830s to Oklahoma Territory during the "Trail of Tears." As in this example, the oldest conchas were cut out in the center; later examples had a bar soldered on the underside for attachment of the discs to the narrow leather strip.

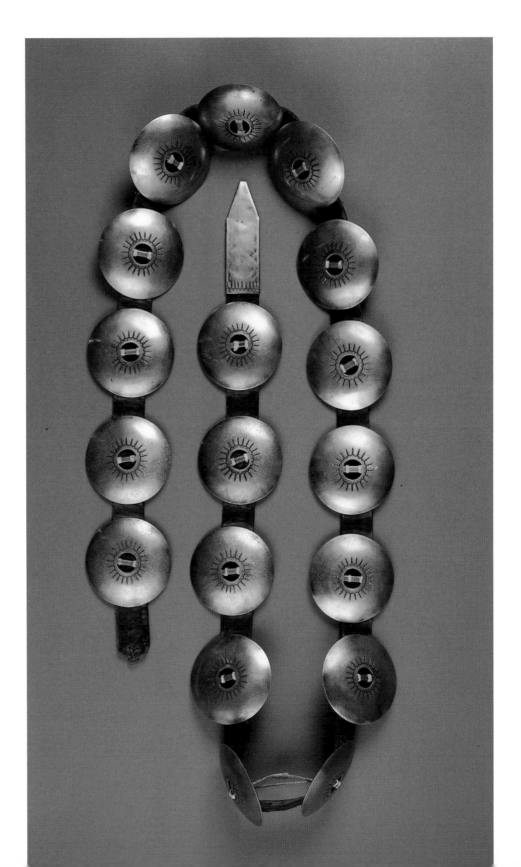

12. Earrings

Northern Plains, mid-19th century
Dentalium shells, leather spacers, metal cones, abalone shells, brass rings
L:7 5/8 in.
Provenance. Bill Helmer, dealer, Golden, British Colombia, n.d.; Painter Collection, 1982

These male Plains Native American earrings are rare, as abalone and dentalium are not indigenous to the Plains region.[1]

___

1. *The only illustrations of this earring style that I am aware of are:* (**1**) *M. F. Schmitt and D. Brown,* Fighting Indians of the West *(1948) 120 (Little Wound, Sioux);* (**2**) *Fighting Indians, 37 (Whistling Elk, Sioux);* (**3**) *The Indians. Time-Life Books,* The Old West Series *(1973) Frontispiece (Many Horns, Sioux);* (**4**) *The Indians, 162 (an unidentified Mandan).* (**5**) *P. R. Fleming and J. Luskey,* The North American Indians in Early Photographs *(1986) 34, no. 2.18 (Iron Nation, Brule Dakota);* (**6**) *The North American Indians, 181, no. 7.3 (Running Antelope, Hunkpapa);* (**7**) *A. L. Bush and L.C. Mitchell,* The Photograph and the American Indian *(1994) 23, no. 25 (The Flying Bird, Sioux);* (**8**) *The Photograph, 25, no. 28 (Coyote);* (**9**) *The Photograph, 37, no. 43 (Lone Wolf, Oglala);* (**10**) *The Photograph, 43, no. 49 (Many Horns, Dakota).*

13. Grizzly Bear Claw Necklace

Great Plains, about 1850
Otter pelt, grizzly bear claws, Venetian glass beads, red trade cloth, hide thong, thread, pigment
L:27 in.
Provenance. Lola Lawrence, Tulsa, n.d.; Paul Gray, dealer, Old Chatham, New York, n.d.; Alex Acevedo, dealer, New York City, n.d.; Painter Collection, 1987.

This necklace consists of 30 Plains grizzly claws attached to a ring of red trade cloth in the Oto tie method. (See N.Feder and M.G.Chandler, *Grizzly Claw Necklaces* (1961) 16, fig. C.) The ring is covered with otter fur, which also drapes down both sides of the back in two flap extensions. Sixty Venetian polychrome beads serve as spacers between the claws, which are four to five inches long when measured from the knuckle to the tip. The claws show evidence of red paint on the underside.

Plains claws are more attractive than the more common mountain grizzly claws because they are considerably longer, and are an attractive light beige rather than the dark brown of the mountain grizzly. They grow longer because the Plains grizzly moves about in a territory featuring a soft sandy soil, while the mountain grizzly tends to wear down his claws while walking on mountainous rocky surfaces. The Plains grizzly became virtually extinct more than 125 years ago.

Grizzly bears are ferocious, can stand about nine feet high, and weigh about a thousand pounds. Their scientific name, *Ursus horribilis*, is most appropriate. Wearing such a necklace implies that the wearer was very brave, as evidenced by his ability to obtain so many claws.

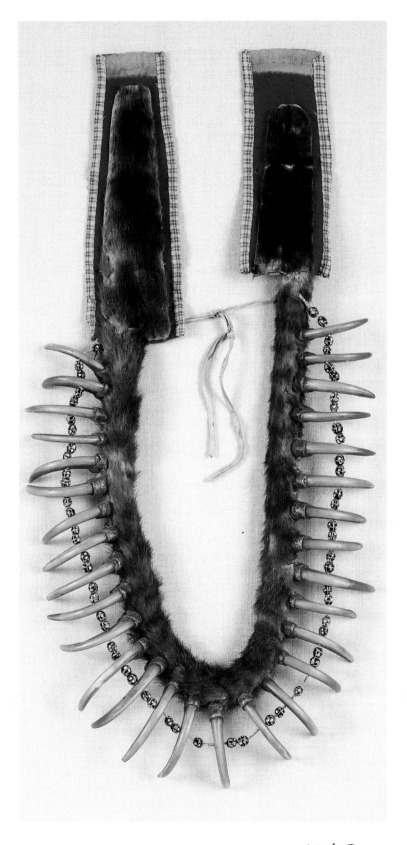

14. Kit Fox Society Necklace

Northern Cheyenne, 19th century
Hide, grizzly bear claws, kit fox tail, snapping turtle tail, metal thimble, metal bell, beads
Provenance. Milford G.Chandler, Detroit, n.d. (Chandler said he obtained it from the Northern Cheyenne); Richard A.Pohrt, Flint, Michigan, n.d.; Alex Acevedo, dealer, New York City, n.d.; Paul Gray, dealer, Old Chatham, New York, n.d.; Painter Collection, 1992.

This necklace was worn only by the bravest warriors, who were members of the Kit Fox Society. The items included on the twisted hide thong are: two Plains grizzly bear claws, the tail of a kit fox, and the tail skin from a snapping turtle. (Assiniboin medicine man, Ken Ryan identified the function of this necklace when he visited the Cincinnati Art Museum on August 8, 1997 to bless the opening of my exhibition, *Tribes of the Buffalo*.) The Kit Fox Society of the Cheyenne tribe was the designated "keeper of the sacred arrows"; this was the tribe's oldest warrior society, dating back to the time before they moved west across the Missouri River. The society's dedication to acting as protectors of their people is exemplified by a song they sang when facing certain death in battle: "Nothing lives long – except the rocks." The Kit Fox Society of the Sioux tribe sang, "I am a Fox – I am supposed to die – if there is anything difficult – if there is anything dangerous – that is mine to do."

15. Sash

Great Lakes area, before 1800
Glass beads, single-ply commercial wool yarn
L:27¼ in.; W:3 3/8 in. (not including fringes)
Provenance. Mark Sykes, England, n.d. (Sykes said that it had been in the James Hooper Collection, England, before 1976); Dick Pohrt Jr., Ann Arbor, Michigan and Jim Ritchie, Toledo, Ohio, dealers, n.d.; Painter Collection, 2001.

This sash was woven with yarn and 9,648 garnet-red and white beads, called "cylindrical, imitation glass-wampum beads." They are slightly smaller than pony beads and some of the red beads are faceted. They were popular between 1760 and 1790, as stated in a letter to me dated June 18, 2001, from noted authority Christian Feest. The human figures woven into the design make it particularly unusual. *(See detail right.)* It probably was worn like a wampum belt and might have been draped over a shoulder or simply carried in the hands to impress others with the owner's importance; it was a prestigious possession.

For similar items, see (**1**) Linden Museum, Stuttgart, garter; (inv. no. 36057, collected by Maximilian zu Wied during his visit to North America in 1832-1834; unpublished; photos of this garter were taken by John Painter on Sept. 11, 2001 in the museum's storage area); (**2**) Winterthur Museum near Zurich, Switzerland; garters and a sash; (collected by Bernhard Rieter in the Niagara Falls area in the early 1800s; unpublished; photos taken by John Painter on Oct. 29, 1997 and Sept. 6, 2001 in the museum's storage area); (**3**) Kneeband; Sauk; present location unknown (inv. no. IV B237, collected by Maximilien zu Wied in 1833; exhibited at Amerika Haus in Berlin, Oct. 6–Nov. 30, 1982, and illustrated in the catalog celebrating the 200th anniversary of Maximilien's birth, p. 20, no. 17); (**4**) British Museum; garter; illustrated in *American Indian Art* Magazine, Winter, 1991, "Woodlands Artifacts from the Studio of Benjamin West 1738-1820," 39, fig. 9.

16. Garter

Cree, about 1800
Blue trade cloth, porcupine quills, hide,
wool, glass pony beads, sinew
L:13 in.
Provenance. James Hooper (1897-1971),
England; Christie's, London, *American
Indian Art from the James Hooper
Collection*, November 9, 1976, Lot 90;
Adelaide DeMenil, New York, n.d.; Will
Channing auction, Santa Fe, August 12,
1990, Lot 165; Painter Collection, 1990.

Published. S. Phelps, *Art and Artifacts of
the Pacific, Africa, and the Americas —
The James Hooper Collection* (1976) 347,
no. 1648 (illus.) and 448 (described).

The woven quillwork on this garter is in a
castellated design: in the shape of turrets
on the top of a castle. On early works such
as this, one often finds a single row of
green or blue-green pony beads at each
end of the quillwork strips.

17. Toiletry Bag

Northern Plains, about 1840
Native tanned hide, red stroud cloth, glass beads, porcupine quills, wood (toggle), sinew, thread
H (pouch): 6 ¼ in.; W (pouch): 4½ in.; L (fringe): 30 in.
Provenance. Paul Gray, dealer, Old Chatham, New York, n.d.; Jim Hart, dealer, Cherry Hill, New Jersey, n.d.; Painter Collection, 1991.

When a man dressed up to visit another tribe or trading post, or to take part in a festive activity at home, he commonly carried a bag containing a trade mirror, face paints, and a comb. This rare bag is a "vanity" item used for cosmetic purposes. A pencil drawing by the Swiss artist Rudolph Friedrich Kurz (1818-1871) depicts an Indian subject with such a bag tied to his wrist while on a visit to Fort Union on the Upper Missouri River in 1851 (see William Wildschut and John C. Ewers, *Crow Indian Beadwork* (1959) fig. 7).[1]

1. *The sketchpad of Rudolph Kurz, a famous Western artist, is housed in the Historisches Museum, Bern, Switzerland.*

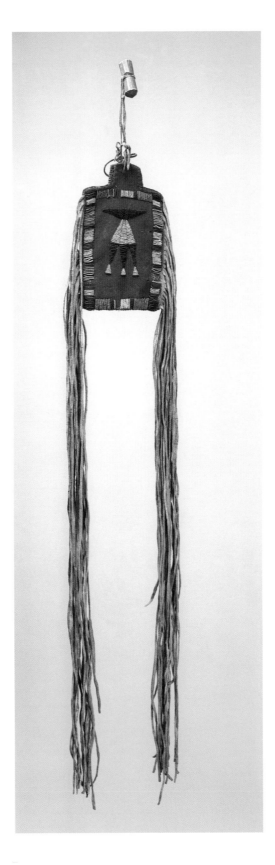
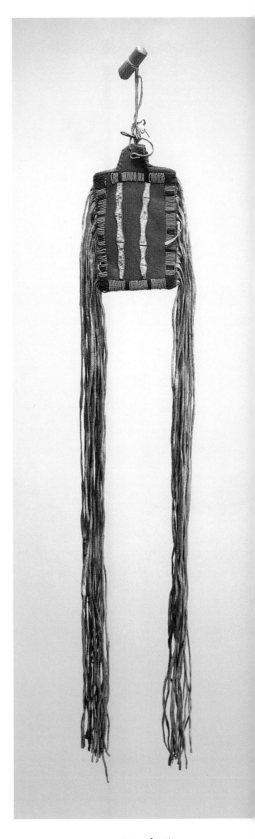

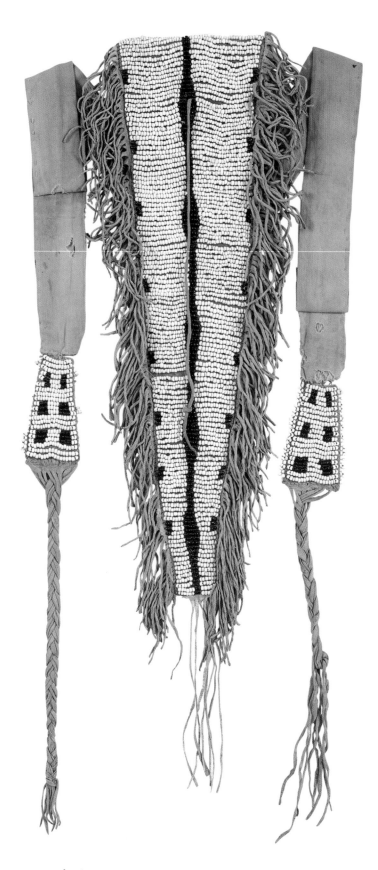

18. Pennant Flap Bag

Northern Plains, possibly Crow, about 1840
Native tanned buffalo hide (body and braided hangs), muslin (belt), glass pony beads, sinew, thread
L (flap): 18 in.; H (bag): 4 in.;
W (bag): 4¾ in.
Provenance. Jim Hart, Cherry Hill, New Jersey, 1986 (obtained in a "write-in" auction); Douglas Deihl, dealer, Florence, Massachusetts; Jim Hart, dealer, Cherry Hill, New Jersey, n.d.; Painter Collection, 1996.
Published. A. Chronister, "Pennant Flap Bags," *Whispering Wind* 23:4 (1990) 4-8.
Reference. In 1996, when Ted Brasser researched this particular bag, he learned that 22 examples have been found in public and private collections, but that this example is one of only four that are decorated with pony beads. The other three examples are located in: (**1**) University of Nebraska State Museum (*American Indian Art Magazine* (Autumn 1984) 52); (**2**) Masco Collection (formerly the collection of the University of Notre Dame, J. Batkin, ed., *Splendid Heritage, Masco Collection* (1995) 30-31); and (**3**) American Museum of Natural History, New York City (unpublished; photo in Painter Collection file).

A variety of bags and pouches substituted for the lack of pockets in Native American garments; this type is named for its distinctive design. A decorated triangular closing flap is edged in fringe and hangs down from the attached muslin belt, hiding the actual billfold-size bag. The flap is pony-beaded with an early, simple design of a black underwater serpent or snake on a white background. The belt is thread-sewn to make a double thickness of muslin because sinew did not lend itself to sewing cloth. Moreover, at that time muslin was more difficult to acquire and more precious than hide. The other parts of this item are made of sinew-sewn buffalo hide. The pony-beaded, decorative ends of the belt have braided fringes, which are usually seen only on Crow Indian artifacts and those of their immediate neighbors.

19. Bag

Cree, about 1780-1820
Native tanned hide, porcupine quills, green
silk thread, sinew
H:9¾ in; W:5¾ in.
Provenance. James Hooper (1897-1971),
England; Christie's, London, *American
Indian Art from the James Hooper
Collection*, November 9,1976, Lot 87;
Adelaide DeMenil, New York City, n.d.;
Will Channing, dealer, auction, Santa Fe,
August 12,1990, Lot 162; Painter
Collection, 1990.
Published. S. Phelps, *Art and Artifacts of
the Pacific, Africa, and the Americas —
The James Hooper Collection* (1976) 347,
no.1581 (illus.) and 446 (described).

This is a good example of fine porcupine-
woven quillwork. The top panel contains
6,786 loops and the bottom panel 6,942,
for a combined total of 13,728 loops.
When this number is divided by the total
surface (27.875 square inches), the average
is 510 loops per square inch, more than
double the number typical for this variety
of quilling. By comparison, the number of
knots per square inch on fine antique
Oriental rugs is 122 on Tabriz rugs and
225 on Kashan rugs.

20. Shoulder Bag

Seminole, about 1840
Wool cloth, glass beads, gold-plated metal
beads, silk ribbon, thread
H (pouch): 8½ in.; W (pouch): 8½ in.;
L (shoulder strap): 55½ in.
Provenance. Private collection, Freeport,
Maine, n.d.; Michael Perez, antique dealer,
New Castle, Maine, n.d.; Morning Star
Gallery, Santa Fe, n.d.; Painter Collection,
1991.
Published. C. Taylor, *North American
Indians: A Pictorial History of the Indian
Tribes of North America* (1997) 8 (illus.);
Michael Johnson, *American Indians of the
Southeast,* Osprey Military, Men-at-Arms,
Series 288 (1995) 20 (illus.).

I nearly refrained from purchasing this bag
because it included shiny "metal" beads
that I normally associate with brass beads
from the late, reservation period. I later
discovered that the 7,000 beads outlining
the design elements of the bag (which vary
from 1.0 to 1.4 mm. in diameter) are metal
plated with 18K gold. The plating is 12
microns (about .0005") thick and encloses
the outside, ends, and hole of a brasslike,
individually cut tube of copper and zinc. I
do not know the source of these beads, but
continuing research has been extensive.
These rare, fascinating gold beads are one
of the most unusual finds in my collecting
experience.

21. Turtle Effigy Bag

Possibly Huron, 18th century
Darkened hide, moose hair, porcupine
quills, sinew
L:10 in.
Provenance. Jim Hart, dealer, Cherry Hill,
New Jersey, 1982; Fred Boschan, Philadel-
phia, 1982; Sotheby's, New York, *Important American Indian Art,* November 29,
1988, Lot 59; Painter Collection, 1988.

The back of this turtle-shaped bag is
missing. The front cover is delicately
embroidered with porcupine quills and
moose hair on darkened hide. The type is
rare, and only three other examples are
presently known in: (**1**) Deutsches
Ledermuseum, Offenbach, (**2**) Museum für
Völkerkunde, Leipzig, ex-Grandduchess
Sophie of Saxe-Weimar, and (**3**) the private
collection of Richard Manoogian, Detroit,
Michigan, who acquired it at Christie's
South Kensington *Auction of Tribal Art,*
June 23,1986, lot 18.
   The function of this bag is not known.
Christian Feest, a respected author of
Native American ethnology and Professor
of Anthropology at Johann Wolfgang
Goethe University, Frankfurt, Germany,
informed me in 1997 that the example in
the Deutsches Ledermuseum was collected
by Johann Baptist Klein of Koblenz. When
Klein donated it to the Senckenberg
Natural History Society in 1825/26, he
recorded it as a tobacco pouch. Klein
never traveled to the United States; he
collected items from French sources who
were known for providing accurate
information about items they acquired.
Because they did not have early books or
other sources that might mislead them
about tribal attribution, their records were
usually correct.

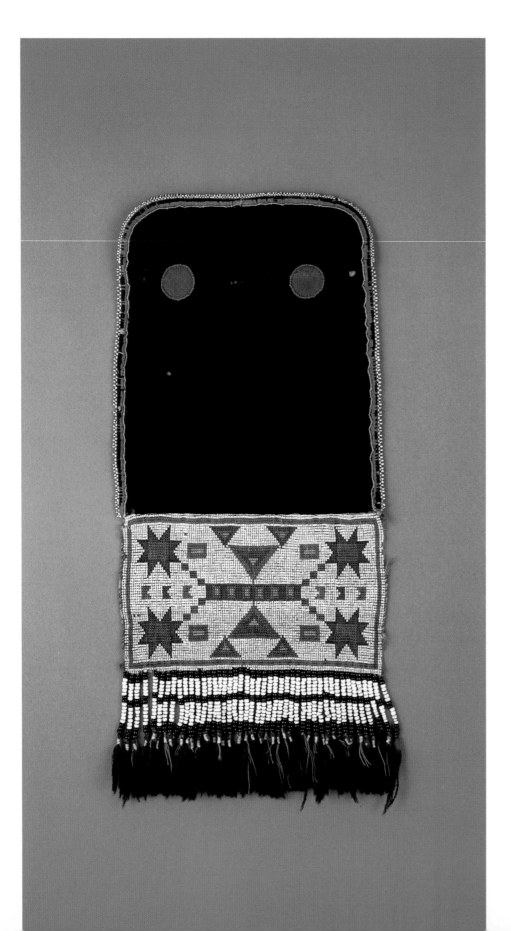

22. Panel Bag

Cree, about 1830
Blue and red trade cloth, commercial cloth lining, glass pony and seed beads, red yarn tassels, red silk ribbon, thread, sinew
H:15½ in; W:7¼ in.
Provenance. Jim Hart, dealer, Cherry Hill, New Jersey, n.d.; Painter Collection, 1982.

On this panel bag, 45 pony-beaded hangs are attached below a loom-beaded panel. The bag portion is composed of dark blue trade cloth with two red cloth circles outlined with light blue beads on each side. An unusual feature of the panel is the use of thread for warp and sinew for weft.

23. Panel Bag

Wasco/Wishram, about 1840
Lac-dyed red trade cloth, green and dark
blue trade cloth, glass beads, wool tassels,
thread, sinew
L:17½ in.
Provenance. Paul Gray, dealer, Old
Chatham, New York, n.d; Painter Collection, 1997.

Panel bags are named for the solid
decorative panel that hangs below the bag
proper. They were made in many varieties
throughout North America, but this is a
very rare example of woven beadwork
from the Plateau area by the Wasco and
Wishram tribes. These tribes lived on the
Columbia River, which acts as a natural
boundary between the states of Washington and Oregon. (For the only known
panel bag with woven beadwork from the
Plateau, see the comments of R.K. Wright,
A Time of Gathering (1991) 73, no. 27.)
In researching the example in the Painter
Collection, Dr. Ted Brasser, a noted scholar
of Native American art, acknowledged in
1997 that this bag was a previously
unknown second example. Bill Holm, a
leading expert on Northwest Coast Indian
artifacts, agreed with this conclusion.

Woven beadwork is very rare. It needs
no backing material and is made with both
warp and double weft threads of sinew,
which hold the beads in horizontal rows.
The black- and pumpkin-colored stylized
human figures in the panel design, which
appear upside down in this example and
therefore "face the wearer," are unique
and are reminiscent of the skeletal human
figures on Wasco/Wishram basketry. The
bag proper is seven inches square and is
made of lac-dyed red trade cloth.

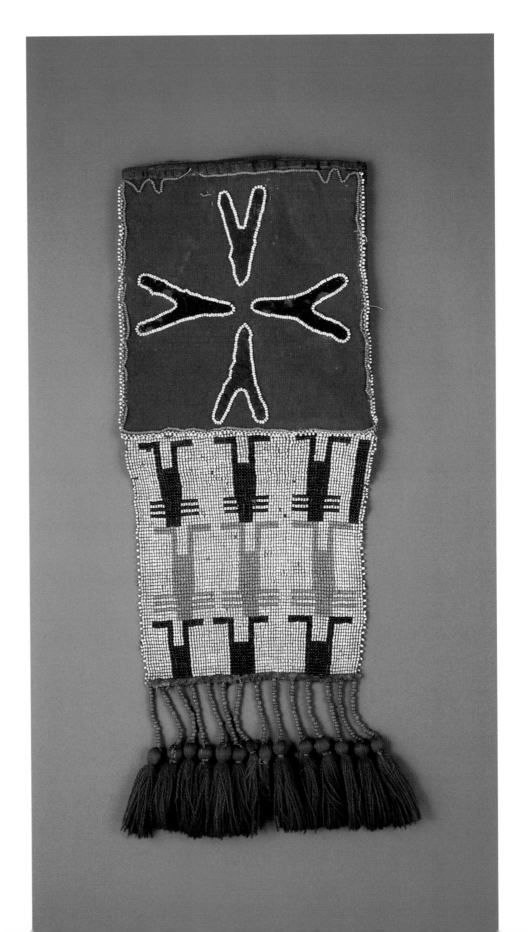

24. Tab Bag

Northeastern Woodlands, 18th century
Darkened thin hide (otter?), porcupine
quills, dyed hair (not human or horse),
metal cones, silk ribbon, sinew
L:21¾ in.
Provenance. Elias Harmon, one of the
original settlers of Mantua, Ohio in 1799;
sold by his great-grandson Olin Harmon
of Ravenna, Ohio, in 1946; Jim Ritchie,
Toledo, Ohio, mid-1980s (purchased at a
Dick Murray auction in Cleveland);
Painter Collection, 1986.

This type of bag, which was made briefly
in the second half of the eighteenth
century, is called a "tab" bag because of
the two rectangular extensions on the
bottom. The rounded upper flaps are worn
tucked under and folded over a belt.
Photos and descriptions of 14 examples
(including this one) are published in C.
Feest, "Tab Pouches of Northeastern
North America," *American Indian Art
Magazine* (Autumn 1997) 34-47. Since
publication, three more have been
identified. They are all made of darkened
hide and are embroidered with porcupine
quills depicting either abstract geometric
symbols or sacred "Spirit Beings." It has
been suggested that such bags have a
relationship to a medicine society known
as the "Black Dance," but there is not
sufficient evidence to substantiate this.
Jonathan Carver's *Travels Through the
Interior Parts of North America in the
Years 1766, 1767, and 1768,* which was
published in 1776, makes reference to the
Pawwaw, or Black Dance. From Carver's
description, it is possible that the dance
may have been associated with a form of
the Midé wiwin (Grand Medicine Society),
although this is certainly not clear. The
quilled designs on the front of the bag
look to me like representations of eight
turtles; the maker's design intentions,
however, are not known.

25. Bag

Kiowa, about 1870
Native tanned hide, glass beads, sinew,
red ocher
H (bag): 8½ in.; L (fringe): 10½ in.
Provenance. Colin Taylor, Hastings,
England (this bag was given to Taylor in
the 1950s by a woman from the Island of
Jersey off the coast of England; her father
had collected it on a trip to the North
American West in the 1880s); Painter
Collection, 2001.
Published. R.T.Coe, *Sacred Circles: Two
Thousand Years of North American Indian
Art* (1977) 183, no. 481.

The fringe on this beaded bag, which is
colored with a red pigment, is very soft and
pliable. On the front there are four
triangular tabs at the bottom. *(See detail
right.)* A bag of this size is not common
among Kiowa artifacts; the Kiowa are best
known for baby cradles and strike-a-light
bags, which are very desirable among
collectors.

The four triangular tabs and the beaded
decoration are very typically Kiowa. The
back has striped and block designs with a
white background, which is very suggestive
of Southern Cheyenne influence. This
mixture of tribal attribution characteristics
is not surprising because the Southern
Cheyenne and Kiowa have been close
neighbors and allies since the historic
Southern Plains treaty of 1840. Since the
last quarter of the nineteenth century they
have lived next to each other on reservation lands in Oklahoma; they have
intermarried and have been influenced by
each other's historic cultural preferences.

Below, detail of beaded design on front of bag. Right, overview of back of bag.

27. Parfleche Cylinder

Nez Perce, about 1870
Rawhide (probably buffalo), buffalo hide strips and fringe, pigment
L :20¾in.; Diameter: 5¼ in.
Provenance. Jim Hart, dealer, Cherry Hill, New Jersey, n.d.; Painter Collection, 1989.

This parfleche cylinder appears to be made of buffalo or elk hide. The long fringes are braided, possibly for portability while fleeing an enemy on horseback. The inside of the top cover flap displays a fascinating provenance record; its significance was brought to my attention by Gaylord Torrence, an authority on parfleche containers at Drake University: "L.H. Jerome/2d Lt./2d Cav Snake Cr./Sept. 30, '77." *(See photo detail to right.)* This historic date was the first day of a final five-day engagement between the Nez Perce and the Second Cavalry, during which Chief Joseph was detained and held prisoner when he came to General Miles under a white flag. His freezing and starving tribe had fought valiantly for months but could not continue. Lieutenant Jerome, who had been sent to the Nez Perce camp to make sure that they had not hidden their guns before surrendering, was captured and held by them in retaliation. The conflict ended in the Bear Paw Mountains of Montana, about 25 miles south of the Canadian border. Chief Joseph and Lieutenant Jerome were exchanged and shook hands on a buffalo robe that had been placed between the two forces. Chief Joseph then made his famous comment: "I will fight no more forever."

26. Parfleche Container

Cheyenne, about 1860
Rawhide, hide thongs, pigment
H:10 in.; W:10 in.
Provenance. Lame Bull, Cheyenne, n.d.; Charles Wickmiller, Oklahoma, 1948; Paul Gray, dealer, Old Chatham, New York, n.d.; Painter Collection, 1989.
Published. W.Coleman, "Art As Cosmology: Cheyenne Women's Rawhide Painting," *The World of Tribal Arts* (Summer 1998) fig. 24 (illus.); I. Nagy, "The Black Came Over the Sun – Lame Bull's Spiritual Oeuvre," *1997 Yearbook of Mora Ferenc Muzeum, Hungary* (1997) 81, fig. 1 (illus.); I. Nagy, "Lame Bull, The Cheyenne Medicine Man," *American Indian Art Magazine* (Winter 1997) 78, fig. 10 (illus.).

This container belonged to Lame Bull, a famous Cheyenne medicine man. A turtle five inches in diameter is painted on the front center, and dragonflies appear on the four corners. Such depictions of animals are extremely rare on parfleche containers, which usually bear geometric designs.

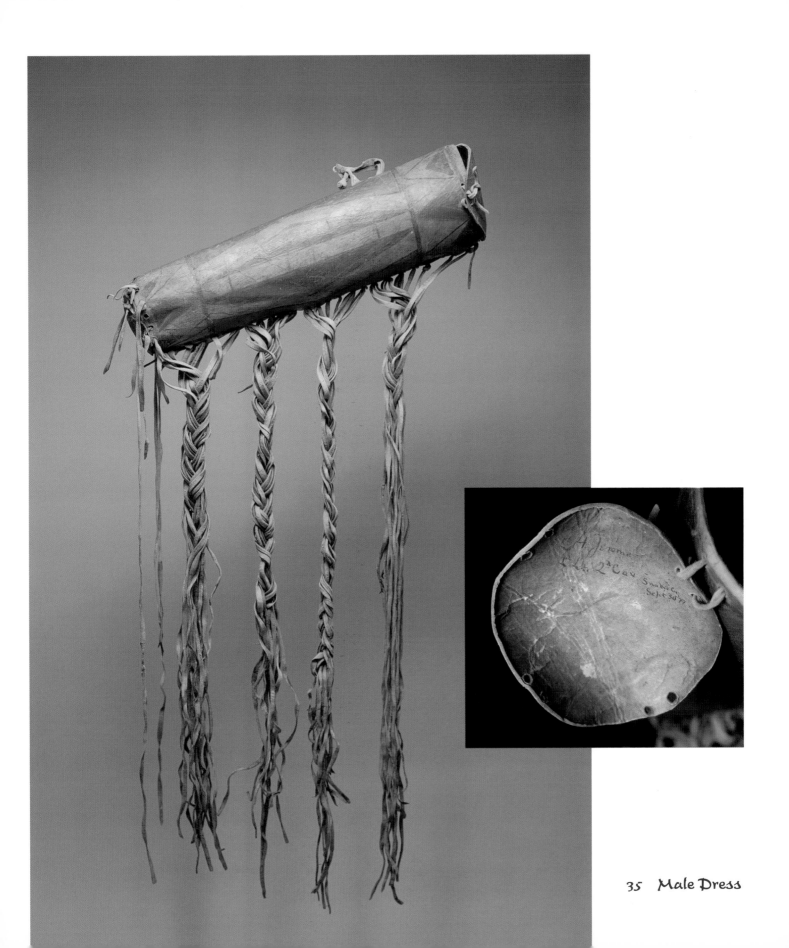

35   Male Dress

28. Tobacco Bag

Cheyenne, about 1820
Native tanned hide, glass pony and crow beads, metal cones, sinew
L: 15½ in.
Provenance. Bob Vandenburg (who claims to have acquired it in eastern Louisiana), Corrales, New Mexico, n.d; Ted Trotta, dealer, n.d.; Alex Acevedo, dealer, New York City, n.d.; Jim Hart, dealer, Cherry Hill, New Jersey, n.d.; Painter Collection, 1990.

This bag is a classic, early, simple design that uses only white and blue beads. The white beads are pony beads and the blue are slightly smaller "real" beads. This particular blue color has become known as "pony trader blue." The top opening has four tabs, and the bottom edge is decorated with 31 metal cone dangles. There are no slat extensions below the bag section. I believe that bags without slats or fringes are several decades older than bags with extensions, but very few pony-beaded bags of this age are available for comparative examination. I find it curious that Karl Bodmer depicted only one tobacco bag in more than 400 surviving drawings. (That one example was not pictured being held or worn by a Native American.)

29. Pipe

Woodlands, 18th century or earlier
Wood (hickory?), lead inlay
L: 15½ in.
Provenance. Paul Gray, dealer, Old
Chatham, New York, n.d.; Painter
Collection, 1995.

This pipe, carved from a single piece of
wood, has a vertical stem orientation and
a human face (carved into the bowl) that
faces the smoker. The pot of the bowl
contains a lead inlay to protect the wood
from the fire of smoking. This pipe is of an
exceedingly rare type, represented by only
a handful of examples. A somewhat
similar pipe may be found in the British
Museum, London (identified as Ojibwa;
ex-Bragg Collection, acquired in 1870
from Ben Pittman of Cincinnati; pub. J.C.
H. King, *First Peoples, First Contacts:
Native Peoples of North America* (1999)
65, no. 63 (illus.)).

37   Male Dress

30. Pipe Stem and Bowl

Upper Missouri River area, about 1800-1820
Wood, porcupine quills, dyed horsehair, sinew, pigment (stem); catlinite, lead inlay (bowl)
L (stem): 36 in.; H (bowl): 3½ in.;
W (bowl): 5 5/8 in.
Provenance. Kurt Schindler (who purchased it in Paris), Freiburg, Germany, 1992; Painter Collection, 1993.

The porcupine quills on this pipe were wrapped around two threads to produce long, continuous "quilled strands" which were wrapped around 11 inches of the stem. The design on the top of the stem includes the depiction of 14 Thunderbirds. The hourglass-shaped designs on the bottom have a symbolic association with the design on the top. A pipe bearing similar designs is located in the Beltrami Collection in Bergamo, Italy (pub. L. Vigorelli, *Gli oggetti indiani raccolti da G. Constantino Beltrami* (1987) 103 (drawing of stem quillwork design)).

The bowl is made of catlinite, a red clay-like mineral found only in a special quarry west of the Falls of Saint Anthony in Minnesota. This is considered to be a sacred place by the Sioux. The red mineral was named for George Catlin, who was one of the first white men to be allowed to visit in 1836. The material is easy to carve with a knife when first taken from the ground, but hardens later. The sides of this bowl have lead inlays, which represent a Thunderbird's pincer claws between rows of connecting diamond symbols relating to underwater monsters. The top of the bowl depicts the Morning Star. The bowl's general shape is like that of other examples of the time period, with a slightly rounded top and a short prow datable to about 1800. The wood of the pipe stem on this example shows evidence of a blue-green paint residue that is associated with other items made during the early nineteenth century or before.

31. Pipe Stem and Bowl

Far left, enlarged detail of thunderbirds on the stem.

Sioux, about 1830
Wood (stem); catlinite, lead inlays (bowl)
L (stem): 23 in.; L (bowl): 5½ in.;
H (bowl): 3 3/8 in.
Provenance. Jim Ritchie, dealer (who obtained it in Wisconsin), Toledo, Ohio, n.d.; Paul Gray, Old Chatham, New York, n.d.; Painter Collection, 1989.

A medicine pipe was among an Indian's most important possessions. The experience of Father Jacques Marquette (1637-1675) confirmed the accuracy of this statement: by merely showing a special peace pipe given to him by the chief of the Illinois Indians, he was saved from attack by hostile Indians at the mouth of the Arkansas River during his search for a route to the Pacific Ocean. "[The Sacred Pipe] is the most mysterious thing in the world. The Scepters of our Kings are not as much respected; for the Savages have such a Deference for this Pipe, that one may call it the God of Peace and War, and the Arbiter of Life and Death" (Father Marquette as quoted at the beginning of Jordan Paper, *Offering Smoke* (1988)).

The stem of this pipe has a carved spiral shape with a very smooth patina, and apparently was painted green at one time. The "barber pole" effect can be accomplished either by carving or by subjecting the straight, flat wood stem to steam generated by boiling water, and then twisting. To determine which method has been used, one must follow the direction of the wood grain. Twisting, a much easier method for achieving this shape, will distort the grain; carving will not. Either method will work unless the wood is too thick to twist. (The term *twisted stem* is often applied in error.) The bowl is of catlinite in the shape of a whiskey keg with hoops encircling it near each end. A similar pipe bowl collected by George Catlin in the 1830s is now housed in the Smithsonian Institution, Washington, D.C. (see J.C.Ewers, *Plains Indian Sculpture* (1986) 99, no. 82 (illus); inv. no. 12, 268).

32. Pipe Stem and Bowl

Eastern Sioux, about 1850-1860
Wood (ash), brass tacks, bone mouthpiece,
pigment (stem); catlinite (bowl)
L (stem): 28¾ in.; L (bowl): 5⅜ in.;
H (bowl): 4 in.
Provenance. Paul Gray, dealer, Old
Chatham, New York, n.d.; Painter
Collection, 1990.

The stem is carved from ash wood, which
was once painted a dark brown. It has
alternating wide and narrow spirals (an
unusual feature), which are painted in
alternating red and brown. Two Morning
Star symbols are incised on the top of the
stem. The bowl has an atypical angular
shape, with no decoration except a slight
ridge at the junction of the horizontal and
the vertical, and no frontal extension. The
bowl slants back toward the smoker at an
acute angle.

33. Rattle

Plains, probably Pawnee, about 1840
Buffalo hide, seeds or pebbles, sinew
(rattle); wood, red trade cloth, commercial
thread (handle)
Diameter (rattle): 6½ in.; L (handle):
5¼ in.
Provenance. Drew Bax, Morrison,
Colorado, mid-1970s; Don Diesner,
Yakima, Washington, n.d.; Morning Star
Gallery, Santa Fe, n.d.; Painter Collection,
1993.

This example is a donut-shaped rattle
made by sewing two pieces of buffalo hide
together with sinew; seeds or pebbles are
trapped inside to make it rattle. The wood
handle is covered with hide and red trade
cloth. Circular rattles were used in both O-
Kee-Pa and Hunka ceremonies.[1] They also
signified membership in an elite group of
Crow warriors called the "Crazy Dog
Society" as well as in the "No Retreat
Society" of other northern Plains tribes.
The history of this rattle suggests that
it is Pawnee.

---

*1. The O-Kee-Pa, a four-day religious
ceremony that was unique to the Mandan
Indians, was an annual dramatization of the
creation of the earth and all living things, and
told of the struggles experienced by the Mandan
in their cultural history. It was first witnessed
and published by George Catlin, whose account
was verified by Prince Maximilian zu Wied. See
C.F. Taylor,* Catlin's O-Kee-Pa *(1996) 12. For
illustrations of similar rattles used during this
ceremony, see G.Catlin,* O-Kee-Pa *(first edition
with* folium reservatum,* 1867) after pp. 16,
17). As N.Bancroft-Hunt states (*Warfare and
the Native American Indian *(1995) 110), "The
circular rattle was an essential requirement of
the Hunka ceremony and of the O-Kee-Pa."
(The Hunka of the Oglala Sioux was a society
of warriors in which an individual was bound
for life in blood brotherhood to another and, by
extension, to all other Hunka; for a description
of the Hunka Society, see* Warfare, *108.)*

**Reservatum, in this instance, refers to three
pages of descriptive narrative that were
included in only a few copies for distribution to
the scientific community: the material was
considered too sexually explicit and too
indelicate for the general reading public of the
Victorian period.*

35. Tomahawk

Northern Plains, about 1875
Wood, brass tacks, iron, silk ribbon,
leather thongs
L:23 5/8 in.
Provenance. Walter Chattin Sr., Wenonah,
n.d. (Chattin claimed that it had belonged
to a Sioux chief, Yellow Hand[1]); Sotheby's,
New York, *Fine American Indian Art*,
May 21, 1996, Lot 143; Morning Star
Gallery, Santa Fe, 1996; Painter Collec-
tion, 1997.
Published. C.F.Taylor, *Native American
Weapons* (2001) 28 (illus.).

This tomahawk is distinguished by a
special feature on both sides of the blade:
it has been etched with pictographic battle
scenes, which tell the story of the owner's
war exploits. On one side, an Indian
sitting on his horse and wearing what
appears to be a Dog Soldier sash shoots a
revolver at a man who is lying on his back
on the ground. The other side depicts a
man wearing a split-horn headdress with a
long feather trailer. Five guns are shooting
at a retreating Indian. A "picture" was
etched on metal by stamping, scratching,
or "rocker engraving," using a tool such
as the front end of a file on the relatively
soft iron blades. Often these blades were
not sharpened because they would not
remain sharp unless a hard steel edge was
inlaid into the blade.

In hand-to-hand combat, Indians had
their own rules concerning the importance
of certain deeds. To "count coup" by
touching an enemy with an object held in
the hand brought greater honor than
killing him: the more coup a man earned,
the higher his status and reputation as a
warrior. In the 1830s, Plains Indians were
taught to create pictographs by visiting
artists such as George Catlin and Karl
Bodmer. There are many examples of
pencil and crayon drawings on paper, and
of earth pigment drawings on buffalo
robes. It was natural for the Indians to
enjoy creating such a permanent record,
because they could not write their history
for lack of an alphabet and written
language. Consequently they had been
forced to rely on spoken words, which
often were repeated around the campfire

34. Shield and Cover

Crow, about 1870 or earlier
Buffalo rawhide, hide carrying thongs
(shield); native tanned deerskin, grizzly
bear ears, black feathers, hair, hide thongs,
red trade cloth, sinew, pigment (cover)
Diameter: 21½ in.
Provenance. Charles Schreyvogel (1861-
1912) Collection, no. 207 (from Hoboken,
New Jersey; ancestors from Stuttgart);
Linden Museum, Stuttgart, inv. no.
113348, L.1604/156; Hermann Seeger,
Stuttgart, 1950s; Painter Collection, 1993.
Exhibited. Ethnographic Museum,
Rotterdam, early 1950s. (Photograph by
Dr. Ted Brasser; copy in the Painter
Collection files.)

This thick buffalo hide shield is slightly
dished; the epidermal upper layer is
heavily patinated. Some of the patination
was cut and scraped away to leave a
decoration of opposing segments of
sunlike designs intersected by a vertical
centerline. It has been suggested that this
could depict the special time of day for
Indians known as "just before dawn"—
the period between dark and sunrise or
between daylight and sunset. Designs on
shields were often created as the result of
"vision quests"; the visions were very
personal and were not to be disclosed.
Therefore, the meaning of this design is
speculative. *(See frontispiece.)*

The shield's cover is made of soft native
tanned deerskin gathered at the back by a
deerskin thong, which is laced through
slits at regular intervals along the edge.
The front is decorated with a central circle
of black feathers flanked by two furry ears
of a grizzly bear. Attached to the center of
the feather circle are a braid of black hair
and a wisp of black horsehair. The grizzly
bear was admired for its enormous power;
anyone displaying a bear's ears would be
respected and feared by association.

at night or in council meetings. There the Indians "counted coup" by retelling the important deeds of past battles.

Tomahawks were much desired by the Indians and became major trade items for the "white man." The most popular of all the types is the pipe tomahawk, where the symbols of war and peace are combined. The handle on this tomahawk has been branded with a heated file and inlaid with brass tacks. It is probably made from ash wood, which was also used for pipe stems because the pith could be burned out from end to end with a hot wire.

———

1. The only Yellow Hand I know of was a Cheyenne killed and scalped by Buffalo Bill Cody on July 17, 1876 in hand-to-hand combat. Buffalo Bill stated that this was "the first scalp for Custer": the general had been killed only about three weeks previously.

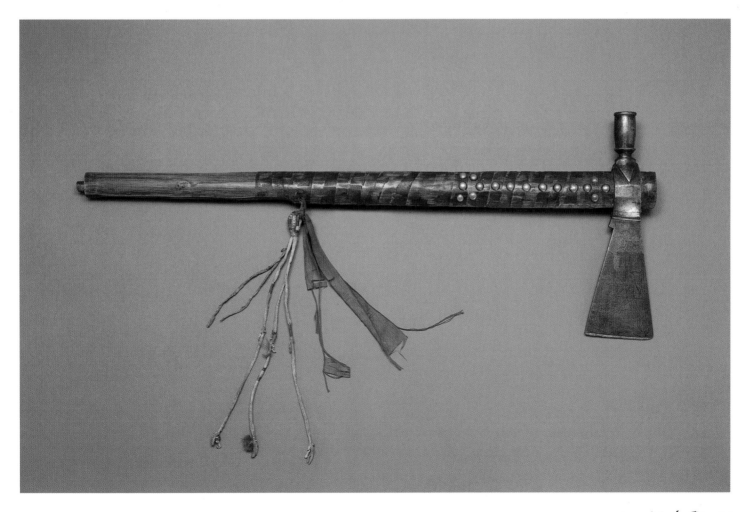

36. Knife and Sheath

Great Lakes area, about 1780
Blackened hide, porcupine quills, sinew
(sheath); horn, wood, metal (knife)
L (sheath): 9 1/8 in.; L (knife): 8 1/8 in.
Provenance. Jim Hart, dealer, Cherry Hill,
New Jersey, n.d. (reportedly from a
southern New York State collection);
Painter Collection, 1984.
Published. C.F. Taylor, *Native American
Weapons* (2001) 42 (illus.).
Exhibited. Plains Indian Museum, Buffalo
Bill Historical Center, Cody, Wyoming,
1990-1992.

The sheath is quilled on hide that probably
was blackened with dye from walnut hulls.
In the eighteenth century, black hide was
preferred as a background field for quills,
moosehair, and beadwork, and we often
find this treatment on items datable to
about 1800 and before. The knife is
distinguished by a finely carved turtle in
raised relief on the end of the horn handle.
The turtle's surface has a rich patina and
reflects unusual artistic talent in the carving.

*End of horn handle with relief of
carved turtle.*

37. Two-Lane Quill-Wrapped Knife Case and Knife

Woodlands, 18th century
Hide, porcupine quills, birch bark slats, sinew (sheath); wood, metal cones and blade, bird quills (knife)
L (sheath): 8¼ in.; L (knife): 9 1/8 in. (not including tassels)
Provenance. Sotheby's, New York, *Important American Indian Art*, November 29, 1988, Lot 68; Arnold Alderman, n.d.; Morning Star Gallery, Santa Fe, 1994 (advertised for sale in *Art & Auction* (February 1994) and in Morning Star Gallery Catalog no. 3); Painter Collection, 1994.
Published. J.Zender and R.Dale, "Great Lakes & Eastern Woodlands Knife Sheaths," *The Book of Buckskinning* VII (1995) 5 (illus.); R.L.Sommer, *Native American Art* (1994) 95 (illus.), circa early 18th century; C.F.Taylor, *Native American Weapons* (2001) 52 (illus.).

The tribal attribution of this knife case is not conclusive. Some say that it originated in the western Great Lakes (possibly Menominee); others designate it as Iroquois (Mohawk), which has a more generic association with Indians for most people. The knife case is called "two-lane" because of a distinctive feature: two narrow vertical quill-wrapped slats of wood, bark, or rawhide with additional quills interwoven to form plaited patterns. Only about 20 examples are known to exist; this one is decorated with bird quills.

The knife is an early (pre-1760) scalping knife with a French mark of a pronged crown on the blade; the British use a rounded crown mark, according to James A.Hanson (personal communication, January 22, 1995). I have another early scalping knife and sheath (not two-lane) with the same mark; Ted Brasser reports a third in the Chichester Museum, England, which was retrieved from the Bunker Hill battlefield by Major William Gaull in 1775.

Enlarged detail of blade showing French mark of pronged crown.

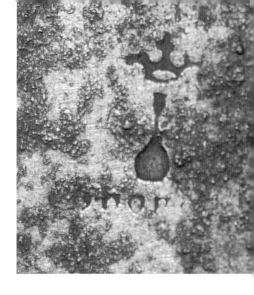

38. Presentation Knife and Sheath

Red River Metis type; Cree, about 1830
Native tanned hide, porcupine quills, birch
bark inner liner, sinew (sheath); horn
(probably Asiatic water buffalo), metal,
bone rivets (knife)
L (sheath): 13 in.; L (knife): 13½ in.
Provenance. Howard Roloff, dealer,
Victoria, British Columbia, n.d.; Kurt
Schindler, Freiburg, Germany, n.d.; Painter
Collection, 1983.
Published. H.Roloff, *American Indian Art
Magazine* (Spring 1980) 88 (advertise-
ment); C.F.Taylor, *Native American
Weapons* (2001) 42 (illus.).
Exhibited. Plains Indian Museum, Buffalo
Bill Historical Center, Cody, Wyoming,
1990-1992.

The knife was made in Sheffield, England;
the handle was carved from water buffalo
horn, which probably came from India.
This type of knife, known as a "dag," a
"stabber," or a "beaver tail," was a
presentation gift given to chiefs by British
officials who were seeking their favor,
much like peace medals and trade guns.
The bottom edge of the handle has neatly
scalloped edges, and the old Sheffield grind
marks extend under the handle, proving
that the blade was ground before blade and
handle were assembled. It has not been
polished or sharpened since.

The sheath, which was made for this
knife by a woman, has flower designs that
are delicately outlined with line quilling on
the front. It features 30 quilled loops across
the front, 22 quilled side hangs, and the
original birch-bark inner liner.

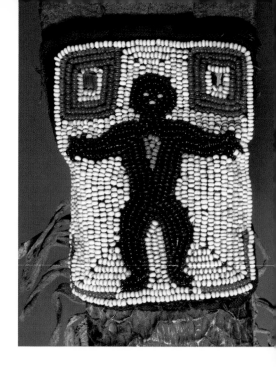

39. Knife and Sheath

Great Lakes area, 19th century
Commercial leather, glass beads, snake
skin, cloth, thread (sheath); metal (knife)
L (sheath): 11½ in.; L (knife): 12 7/8 in.
Provenance. Paul Gray, Old Chatham,
New York, n.d.; Painter Collection, 1996.
Published. Colin F.Taylor, *Native Ameri-
can Weapons* (2001) 50 (illus.).

This sheath has some interesting characteristics, which suggest a relationship with a
secret or sacred organization such as the
Midé Wiwin Society: the use of snakeskin;
the contours of the human figure; the
depiction of a heart on the chest (could
this be connected with the small seashell
"shot into" a Midé initiate?); and the
beaded squares in two corners above the
man's figure (could this indicate a second-
phase initiate?). (See W.J.Hoffman, "The
Midé Wiwin or Grand Medicine Society of
the Ojibwa," *7th Annual Report of the
Bureau of Ethnology, 1885-1886,* 167-
168.) A search of the literature has turned
up approximately 20 examples of a human
figure such as the one depicted here. These
often seem to denote a "being" with
special spiritual or shamanistic powers.

The knife probably was made by a
blacksmith using parts from a tomahawk
and the barrel of a lightweight trade gun.

Knife and sheath above, with detail top left.

40. Knife

Great Lakes area, early 19th century
Wood, lead or pewter inlays, metal blade
L:11 3/8 in.
Provenance. Paul Gray, dealer, Old
Chatham, New York, n.d.; Painter
Collection, 1998.

This unique knife appears to be very old
and apparently has been sharpened many
times. The wooden handle contains inlays
of lead or pewter, with three Thunderbirds
on one side and designs depicting underwater creatures on the other.

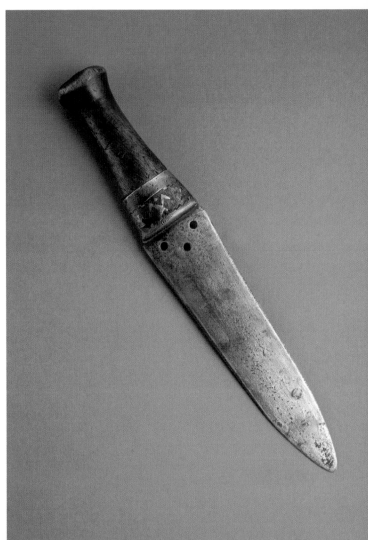

41. Dress

Blackfeet, about 1870
Native tanned hide, red and black stroud
cloth, glass pony and seed beads, bone
(simulated elk teeth), sinew, thread
L:46½ in.
Provenance. Jim Hart, dealer, Cherry Hill,
New Jersey, n.d.; Painter Collection, 1984.
Published. C.Taylor, *Yupika – The Plains
Indian Woman's Dress* (1997) 55 (illus.).
As Taylor states, "The red and black cloth
inserts on each side of the bottom are
found on a number of Blackfeet dresses."

This pony-beaded dress is decorated on the
front and back with a total of 20 simulated
elk teeth of carved bone. These replicas
show remnants of a dark-brown paint,
which was meant to simulate tartar.
Because each elk had only two teeth (the
upper canines or milk teeth) that were
favored for decoration, fake elk teeth of
carved bone were often used in substitution.

42. Dress

Plateau, probably Yakima, about 1875
Mountain sheep hide, glass pony beads,
sinew. L:52 in.
Provenance. Louis Comfort Tiffany (1848-
1933), New York City, n.d.; Parke-
Bernet Galleries, New York City, auction,
September 24-28,1946, Lot 505, sold for
the Tiffany Foundation; Skinner, Bolton,
Massachusetts, auction, January 15,1988,
Lot 96; Sotheby's, New York, *Important
American Indian Art*, May 19,1998, Lot
136; Painter Collection, 1998.

This woman's dress of finely tanned
mountain sheep hide is decorated with
pony beads. The size and number of beads
make the dress very heavy to wear for any
extended period; it weighs 10 pounds,
3½ ounces. The red-and-white bead color
combination creates a soft, attractive
earth tone.

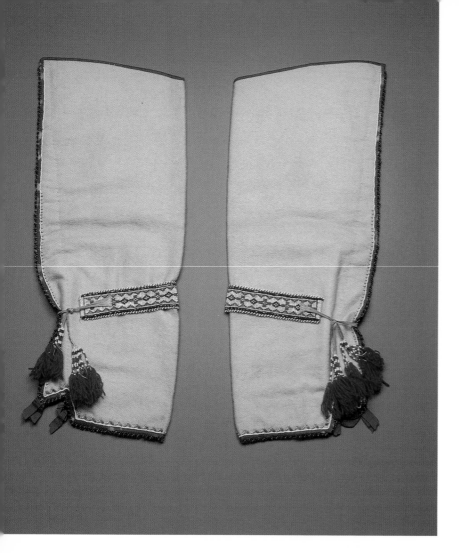

43. Leggings

James Bay area, Cree, before 1830
Hudson's Bay Company wool blanket
material, hide, pony and seed beads, red
wool hangs, silk cloth, sinew
L:23 in.
Provenance. Paul Gray, dealer, Old
Chatham, New York, n.d.; Painter
Collection, 1991.

These leggings are made of heavy woven,
beige Hudson's Bay blanket material edged
with blue silk. They are sinew-sewn with
black, blue, and pink pony beads. According to Richard A. Pohrt, Ted Brasser,
Benson Lanford, Paul Gray, and Tom
Connin, the construction of the garters is
unique. The beads are strung on a sinew
weft, which passes through each bead
twice. The warp is leather cut extremely
fine, which passes between the two weft
strands. The warp must have been made
with belly leather from the animal to
enable stretching to such a fine consistency.
The hide probably was sliced very thin
with a sharp knife while two people held it
taut, then wet and stretched further until it
was no thicker than thread. A high degree
of craftsmanship was required to make
these warps before the availability of
precision cutting machines.

45. Belt

Northern Plains, about 1860-1870
Commercial leather, metal conchas, metal buckle, hide thong
L:41 in.; Diameter (conchas): 2 3/8 in.
Provenance. Graf Karl von Linden, Stuttgart, n.d.; Linden Museum, Stuttgart, July 4,1906; [1] Hermann Seeger, Stuttgart, 1954; Painter Collection, 1999.

This woman's belt was made from a soldier's cartridge belt. The places where the leather was formerly stitched to make cartridge loops are quite evident. These loops have been cut away to accommodate 12 German silver conchas.[2] The use of looped cartridge belts by cavalry began in 1866. Although favored by the men who used them, leather belts were not approved by the army because the acid in the leather acted on the copper in the shells, producing verdigris. This caused the cases to stick in the loops and, after firing, in the chamber of the carbine. Many troopers thus made up cartridge belts for themselves. It seems logical to assume that this belt was taken from a dead soldier.

---

1. The records at the Linden Museum, Stuttgart, indicate that this belt was given on July 4, 1906 by Graf (equivalent of an English Earl) Karl von Linden. It was assigned the five-digit number 44658, which is shown in white ink on the inside of the belt along with the inscription "v. Linden." (The numbering was changed to a six-digit system in the early 1900s, when the museum was renamed for von Linden.)

2. German silver is an alloy of copper, zinc, and nickel and is a cheaper imitation of silver. See R.Conn, Circles of the World (1982) no.77. As Conn remarks: "Circular silver ornaments, or conchas, which probably derived from prehistoric Southeast shell discs, were introduced to Plains smiths by displaced Southeast tribes relocated in Oklahoma in the late 1830s. Among the new uses Plains artists devised for the ornaments were hairplates...As the custom of wearing hairplates declined in the 1870s, conchas were mounted on leather belts."

44. Moccasins

Huron, about 1800
Darkened deerhide, moosehair, cloth, sinew, thread
L:8¾ in.
Provenance. Anthony Schoeller, Paris, n.d.; Kurt Schindler, Freiburg, Germany, 1986 (purchased through Anthony Meyer, dealer, Paris); Painter Collection, 1986.

Before 1800, it was customary to dye hide very dark (almost black) with stain made from walnut or hickory hulls, wild grapes, or the bark of the alder tree. The decoration on the ankle flap of these moccasins extends completely around the heel area and is not split in the back; this is an uncommon feature. The small size and the type of these moccasins indicate that they were made for a woman. Embroidery using moosehair was taught to Huron Indians of Lorette by the Ursuline nuns in Quebec.

46. Hair Drop

Probably Wasco, about 1840
Dentalium shells, glass beads, rawhide,
metal coins and military buttons, sinew
H:13½ in.; W:4 in.
Provenance. Dale E. Heinemann, dealer,
Santa Fe, n.d.; Painter Collection, 1989.

This woman's hair ornament consists of
dentalium shells, large beads in bright red
and blue, five Chinese coins, an English
coin, and an Irish farthing dated 1780. It
also includes three military buttons from
Haiti (under French control in the early
1800s), which say *je renais de mes cendres*,
"I am reborn from my ashes."

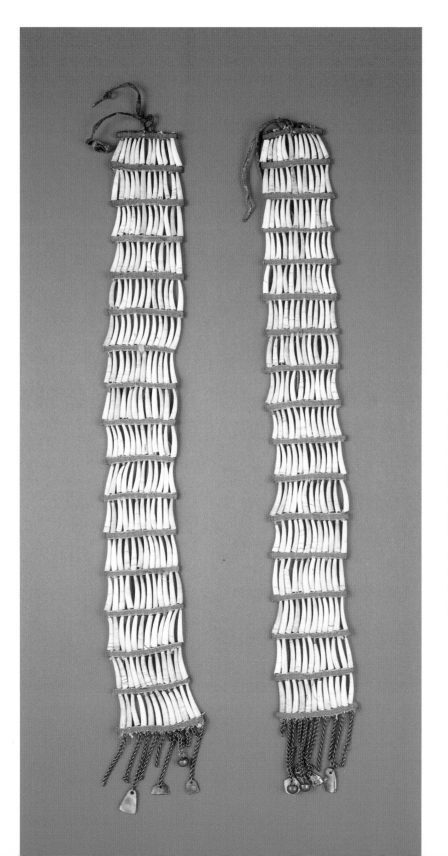

47. Earrings

Northern Plains, 19th century
Dentalium shells, abalone shells, leather,
metal chains, sinew
L:18 in. (not including hangs)
Provenance. Drew Bax, Morrison, Colorado, n.d. (Bax's records indicate that he
bought this item from "Tilton" and that
the earrings are Blackfeet); Paul Gray,
dealer, Old Chatham, New York, n.d.;
Painter Collection, 1993.

Each earring consists of 17 rows of
dentalium shells, which are strung on
sinew and separated by leather spacers.
Long earrings such as these were a "high
fashion" accessory and were rare.

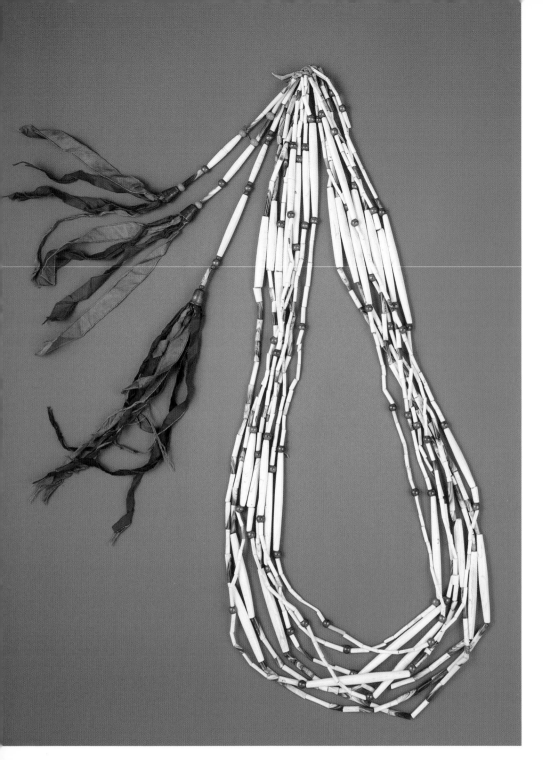

48. Necklace

Winnebago, probably early 19th century
White whelk seashells, purple quahog
clamshells, glass and metal spacer beads,
metal thimbles, silk ribbon, hide
L:about 24 in. (when worn)
Provenance. Descended in the Decora (De
Kaury, De Cora, Decorah) family of the
Winnebago;[1] Sarah Lonetree Lyons,
Decora family, n.d.; Ramona Morris,
dealer, Delaplane, Virginia, 1984 (*American Indian Art Magazine* (Winter 1984) 64
(advertisement)); Painter Collection, 1985.

This rare wampum necklace, worn by a
woman, is actually two necklaces worn
together. One is a single long strand of shell
hair pipes, which are looped to make five
strands; the other has been looped to make
three strands. Wampum was acquired by
trade with coastal tribes, who made white
wampum from the central column of the
whelk seashell and purple wampum from
the violet spot on certain hard-shell or
quahog clamshells. Wampum was rarely
used for decorative necklaces because of its
great value: the Indians attached great
importance to its spiritual power. More
than a unit of barter exchange, wampum
was fashioned into belts that symbolized
the wearers' laws and tribal history.

Wampum shells were made by drilling
the center holes from each end until they
met in the middle. This task was difficult

because the tools that were available to the Indians were less than precise. I have X-rays of this necklace, which confirm this method of drilling.

1. See P.Radin, "The Winnebago Tribe," 37th Annual Report of the Bureau of American Ethnology (1915-1916) 49-69. Decora was the name of a Frenchman who, early in the eighteenth century, was one of the first white men to visit the Winnebago in their original home near present-day Green Bay, Wisconsin. Decora taught them to make and use tools, married the chief's daughter, Glory of the Morning, and fathered two sons. Descendants of French blood from the Decora family have always been the chosen chiefs of the Winnebago. I have a photo of Annie Decorah White (Fresh Tracks), the wife of Big Wave, wearing this necklace, circa 1930. (This photo is a copy of the original, which is located in the Milwaukee Public Museum.)

49. Necklace

Plateau, 19th century
Dentalium shells, glass beads, hemp
L:about 22 in.
Provenance. Paul Gray, dealer, Old Chatham, New York, n.d.; Painter Collection, 2001.

This necklace consists of 22 strands of half-inch-long dentalium shells, separated by some blue but mostly red pony beads and strung on twisted hemp. This style of necklace is very rare.

50. Parfleche

Cheyenne, about 1860
Rawhide (remnants of light-colored hair),
hide closure thongs, pigment
H:28½ in.; W:16 in.
Provenance. Charles E. Seese, West
Virginia, n.d.; Lynn Munger, dealer,
Angola, Indiana, 1986; Rich Edwards,
Toledo, Ohio, 1986; Painter Collection,
1986.

A parfleche is a container of folded or
sewn rawhide with decorative painted
designs on the exposed surfaces. Rawhide
is not tanned; therefore it is not pliable
like tanned hides, which are used to make
most Native American leather items. The
present example is a rectangular envelope,
probably made of cowhide, which retains
some small areas of light hair. This type of
container is the Native American equivalent of a suitcase and was used to store
many items, including food and clothing.
The word *parfleche* comes from the French
pare une flèche, "turns an arrow."
Cheyenne parfleche decoration has a
translucent sharpness with delicate
outlining; the Cheyenne are the only tribe
that used turquoise as the main paint
pigment. This was very effective, and these
examples are considered the finest in
design and execution.

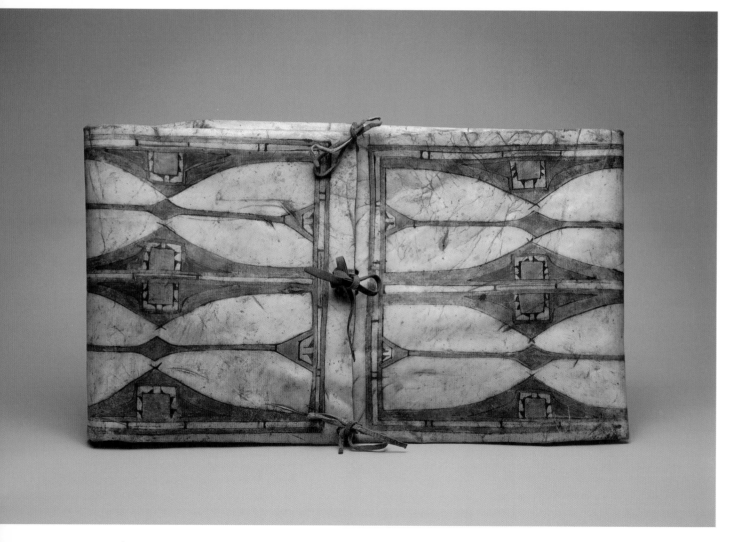

51. Baby Cradle

Iroquois, Mohawk, about 1850
Wood, rawhide strips, pigment
H:30 in.
Provenance. Sotheby's, New York, *Fine American Indian Art*, October 21,1994, Lot 125; Painter Collection, 1994.

This cradle consists of a wooden board with a carved head protector in front and a footrest to hold the child in place. The back is intricately carved and painted with designs of birds: one group resembles peacocks, and four smaller birds seem to be eating fruit from a flowering tree. This design is highly symbolic: the roots of the tree spread in the four cardinal directions, and clan effigies often are carved and painted at the base. When placed in this cradleboard, the child was secure and was tied symbolically to the traditions of the tribe. For an almost identical cradleboard, see T.Hill and R.W.Hill Sr., eds., *Creation's Journey* (1994) 23, identified as one of the masterworks from the Smithsonian's National Museum of the American Indian.

52. Baby Cradle

Kiowa, late 19th century
Wood, rawhide, native tanned hide, shoe
buttons, glass beads, thread
L (cradle): 30 in.; L (slats): 43 5/8 in.
Provenance. Charles E. Seese, West
Virginia, n.d.; Lynn Munger, dealer,
Angola, Indiana, 1986; Painter Collection,
1986.

For Tahdo Ahtone (1879-1966), probably
the maker of this cradle, see B.A.Hail,
*Gifts of Pride and Love – Kiowa and
Comanche Cradles* (2000) 82-87. Ahtone
was reported to have made eight full-size
cradles and many toy cradles. She pio-
neered the oak leaf design and laced the
covers to the boards in a distinctive
fashion, joining them with rawhide thongs
through nine holes at each end. This cradle
is consistent with her design and construction techniques. The beads are thread-
sewn in an asymmetrical design using
midnight blue and green on a teal-blue
background.

53. Knife Sheath

Western Ojibwa (Chippewa), about 1820
Red trade cloth, glass beads, porcupine
quills, feathers, birch bark inner liner,
ribbon material, silk tassels, thread, sinew
L:10½ in.
Provenance. James Hooper (1897-1971),
England; Christie's, London, *American
Indian Art from the James Hooper
Collection,* November 9, 1976, Lot 79;
Arthur Speyer, Wiesbaden, Germany,
1976; Bill Helmer, dealer, British Colum-
bia, 1982; Painter Collection, 1982 (see W.
C.Sturtevant, "Documenting the Speyer
Collection," *Studies in American Indian
Art – A Memorial Tribute to Norman
Feder* (2001) 162-186, which documents
the acquisition of this item by the Painter
Collection).
Published. S.Phelps, *Art and Artifacts of
the Pacific, Africa, and the Americas –
The James Hooper Collection* (1976) 348,
no. 1702 (illus.) and 449 (described).
Exhibited. Plains Indian Museum, Buffalo
Bill Historical Center, Cody, Wyoming,
1990-1992.

On this sheath, red trade cloth forms the background for a woven quillwork panel across the upper front. This item has two original birch-bark inner liners and tiny beaded decorations, along with large milk-glass barrel-shaped ovoid beads on the suspensions.

54. Ladle

Probably Woodlands, about 1800
Wood
L: 10 3/8 in. (top to bottom)
Provenance. Paul Gray, dealer, Old Chatham, New York, n.d.; Painter Collection, 1999.

The top of the handle features an artistically sculpted otter that looks back over its shoulder. The right-hand edge of the handle has been worn away in a curving pattern, giving the appearance of many years of use. When the ladle is held in the right hand and its use is simulated with a wooden bowl, it mixes, stirs, and serves with a circular motion that causes the handle to rub against the rim of the bowl in exactly the areas that are worn away. The shape of the protruding perch on which the otter sits produces a configuration that keeps the handle from sliding down into the bowl, when the ladle is resting on the side of the bowl.

55. Dress

Southern Cheyenne, about 1880
Native tanned hide, cowrie shells, glass
beads, metal cones, ocher dye, sinew
L:33 in.
Provenance. James Hooper (1897-1971),
England; Christie's, London, *Tribal Art*,
June 23,1986, Lot 12 (consigned by one
of Hooper's granddaughters); Alex
Acevedo, New York City, who sold it to
Laura and Richard Fisher, October 24,
1986; Howard Roloff, Victoria, British
Columbia, December 1, 1990; Painter
Collection, 1990.
Published. S.Phelps, *Art and Artifacts of
the Pacific, Africa, and the Americas –
The James Hooper Collection* (1976) 341,
no. 1618 (illus.) and 447 (described); C.
Taylor, *Yupika – The Plains Indian
Woman's Dress* (1997) 41 and color cover
image. (*Yupika* in Sioux means "to dress
up nicely, to clothe oneself well.")

This young girl's dress is decorated on the
front and back with 551 cowrie shells,
which are indigenous to the warm waters
off the Pacific Coast. These trade items
replaced elk teeth as decorative ornaments
when the latter became difficult to obtain.

56. Dress

Crow, about 1870
Red stroud cloth (body), beige cloth trim
(neck, cuffs, and hem), elk teeth, bone,
thread, hide thongs
L:27 in.
*Provenance. American Indian Art Maga-
zine* (Spring 1996) 111 (advertised by
James B. Mighton, Calgary, Alberta); Paul
Gray, Old Chatham, New York, n.d.;
Painter Collection, 1996.

This young girl's dress is made of red
stroud cloth, a coarse woolen cloth or
blanket textile named after the manufac-
turing center Stroud in Gloucestershire,
England. It is decorated with a total of
327 "elk teeth," of which only 45 are real;
the remainder are replicas in bone. Because
each mature elk has only two upper
canines, or "milk teeth," these were very
much in demand by the Indians; the Crow
in particular used them as decorative
ornaments. It would have taken many
years to accumulate enough real teeth, so
it was common to carve imitation teeth
from bone. Paul Gray and I studied the
teeth on this dress with the help of a
magnifying glass to determine which
examples were real and which were
imitations in carved bone. Identification
was difficult because the imitation teeth
were expertly carved and the real teeth
showed some knife carving and file marks
(including drilled holes for attachment).

57. Mittens

Kutchin, about 1850
Native tanned hide, porcupine quills,
sinew. L:6 in.
Provenance. James Hooper (1897-1971),
England; Christie's, London, *Tribal Art*,
July 4,1990, Lot 150; John Molloy, Santa
Fe, 1990; Painter Collection, 1990.
Published. S. Phelps, *Art and Artifacts of
the Pacific, Africa, and the Americas –
The James Hooper Collection* (1976) 346,
no. 1642 (illus.) and 448 (described).

These child-size mittens are connected by a
quilled thong 25 inches long, which is
meant to pass through the inside armholes
to keep the mittens from being lost.

58. Doll Cradle

Huron, 18th century
Wood, porcupine quills, metal crosses,
cloth ribbon material, sinew
H:6½ in.
Provenance. James Hooper (1897-1971),
England; Christie's, London, *Important
Tribal Art*, June 23,1992, Lot 126; Painter
Collection, 1992.
Published. S. Phelps, *Art and Artifacts of
the Pacific, Africa, and the Americas –
The James Hooper Collection* (1976) 336,
no. 1588 (illus.) and 447 (described).

The small size, the decorative carving of
the board around the periphery on the
front and back, and the six small metal
crosses on the woven quillwork head
protector make this a unique and extraor-
dinary example of a doll cradle of great age.

64 *Children's Dress*

59. Doll Cradle

Cree, about 1775-1800
Wood, trade cloth, porcupine quills, glass
beads, metal cones, dyed horsehair, thread,
sinew, pigment
H (board): 14 3/8 in.; W (board): 6 5/8 in.
Provenance. Phillips, de Pury Luxembourg,
London, *Tribal Art*, October 25, 2001, Lot
1; Painter Collection, 2001.

The head protector and a strip across the
back have woven quillwork panels. On
three sides of the front bottom, a plaited
quill design is sewn to the cloth cover, and
many pony bead and quill-wrapped hangs
are present. The back top center of the
wood board has two triangular cutouts;
Cath Oberholtzer, an expert on Cree
material with the Canadian Museum in
Ontario, believes that this portion of the
cradle is in an iconic Thunderbird form.
The British Museum has a Cree doll cradle
of this general type, acquired about 1740
by John Potts while he was working for
the Hudson's Bay Company. It is now
quite plain and has lost most of its former
decoration, but also has the two triangular
cutouts on the back top center of the
wood board.
  Only a few Cree doll cradles can be
dated to around 1800. It is therefore
appropriate to compare other types of
related Indian artifacts from the same area
and time: (**1**) two female dolls in the
Horniman Museum, London; see *American Indian Art Magazine* (Winter 1984),
cover of anniversary issue, circa 1790; (**2**)
two female dolls sold at Christie's, South
Kensington, *Tribal Art*, April 4, 1989, Lot
280, circa 1800. The smaller doll is in a
cradle with some design elements that are
similar to those shown here; (**3**) a male and
a female doll, plus a doll cradle, in the
Rosalie Whyel Museum of Doll Art,
Bellevue, Washington. That cradle, like the
present specimen, has beaded hangs on the
front and back, but no quilling. The Whyel
cradle is decorated with a cutout on the
top center of the back, which resembles an
iconic Thunderbird with beaded wing
feathers; (**4**) a Parklands Cree type shirt,
early eighteenth century, located in the
Kungl. Livrustkammeren, Stockholm; see

Glenbow Museum, *The Spirit Sings* (1988)
108, no. 98. Note the red and black
painted roundel at the center of the chest,
which is very much like the painted design
on this cradle. Also, the horizontal painted
red and black triangles on the shirt are like
the triangles of red and black paint on the
back of the cradle; (**5**) the quilling and
beading on the Cree costume (cat. no. 1
in this exhibition), which possesses many
characteristics in common with this
doll cradle.

Left, front view of doll cradle.
Below, rear view.

60. Doll Cradle

Crow, about 1870
Wood, hide, red trade cloth, glass beads, thread
L (cradle): 24 in.; L (doll): 12 in.
Provenance. Howard Roloff, dealer, Victoria, British Columbia, n.d.; Painter Collection, 1987.

This typical Crow doll cradle contains an interesting doll wearing a red trade cloth dress with white bead decorations. The beads are meant to simulate elk teeth or cowrie shells that normally would decorate real, adult dresses.

61. Doll Cradle

Kiowa, about 1880
Wood, hide, glass beads, brass tacks,
thread
L (cradle): 12½ in.; L (boards): 19 3/8 in.
Provenance. Paul Gray, dealer, Old
Chatham, New York, n.d.; Painter
Collection, 1992.

Kiowa cradles are sought after because of
the esthetic appeal of their design and color
combinations. Typically the design is
asymmetrical, with different colored
backgrounds and complementary colors
used in the curvilinear figures on the right
versus the left side. The curvilinear figures
are not known in Kiowa bead embroidery
on other types of items; this suggests that
these designs may represent influences from
other midwestern tribes who later relocated
near the Kiowa in Oklahoma. The Kiowa
also outlined all the figures and used
straight lines of beads in filling in the
design shapes. They used "earth-tone"
colors that are soft and pleasing to the eye,
such as garnet red, turquoise blue, laven-
der, greasy yellow, and teal.

62. Pair of Dolls

Micmac, about 1840-1850
Wood, cloth, hide, metal, thread, pigment
H (male): 18 in; H (female): 15 in.
Provenance. Collected in Canada by Lt. Col. Thomas Dyneley, C.B., A.D.C. to Queen Victoria (according to records of the Royal Ontario Museum, Toronto, Dyneley commanded the Royal Artillery in Ottawa, Montreal, and Quebec 1848-1852; he returned to England in 1852); Amy Dyneley, daughter; Marg Vigors, née Dyneley, niece; Dreweatts auction catalog, Berkshire, England, January 21, 1987, Lot 302; Michael Graham-Stewart, dealer, London, 1987; Painter Collection, 1987.

These dolls have artistically carved and painted wood heads that resemble those of actual people. The woman's face appears to have a "crackled" surface similar to a gesso layer, or this may be aged varnish. The bodies have articulated arms and legs, which are attached with wood pegs. The female wears a typical Micmac hat, while the male carries a wood gun, a powder horn, a knife and sheath, and a pipe bowl.

63. Pair of Dolls

Sioux, about 1875
Cloth, hide, glass beads, porcupine quills,
sinew, simulated hair (?)
H (male): 11¾ in.; H (female): 10¾ in.
Provenance. Paul Gray, dealer, Old
Chatham, New York, n.d.; Painter
Collection, 1991.

Doll pairs are not common. Both dolls in
this example have cloth bodies with hide
costumes, and round hide heads with
braided hair. The male is decorated with
quills; the female, with beads.

64. Female Doll

Iroquois, about 1850
Goatskin, blue trade cloth, patterned
commercial cloth, papier-mâché, glass
beads, thread, yarn
H:10 in.
Provenance. Sotheby's, New York, *Fine
American Indian Art*, May 21,1991, Lot
105; Painter Collection, 1991.

This doll has a goatskin body, wooden
limbs, and papier-mâché head, and wears a
patterned cloth dress, beaded hide
moccasins, blue trade cloth leggings, and
an apron. The sash around the waist
simulates a woven band with interspersed
beads. Mary Krombholz, a Cincinnati
friend and author of books and articles
about dolls, believes that this doll's head
and body were produced during the first
half of the nineteenth century at Andreas
Voit's papier-mâché factory in the
Thüringian forest in Germany. An Iroquois
Native American dressed the doll in their
native costume.

65. Female Doll

Sioux, about 1880
Hide, blue stroud cloth, glass beads, metal
sequins, human hair, thread, sinew,
pigment. H:17 in.
Provenance. Ken Canfield, dealer, Santa
Fe, n.d.; Painter Collection, 1980.

This doll, which has dark brown human
hair, wears a dress of midnight-blue stroud
cloth with a light gray border at the hem
and cuffs. This undyed selvage has small
holes along the edge, which occur when
the cloth is fastened over pins along the
borders during the dying process. The pin-
holes are a sign that the stroud cloth was
made quite early; by holding the edge of
the cloth up to the light, one can see
whether such holes are present. The dress
is decorated with hand-cut sequins.